THE HERO IN ME

TEACHER'S GUIDE

By Miriam Aronin and Judy Dick

Foreword and Activities by Assaf Gamzou
The Museum of the Jewish People at Beit Hatfutsot

BEHRMAN HOUSE
www.behrmanhouse.com/hero

Contents

Chapter 1 by Judy Dick
Introduction and Chapters 2–5 by Miriam Aronin

Published by Behrman House, Inc.
Millburn, New Jersey 07041
www.behrmanhouse.com

ISBN 978-1-68115-057-4

Design by Tim Holtz
Project Editor: Alef Davis

Printed in the United States of America

9 8 7 6 5 4 3 2 1

Foreword

MUSEUM OF THE
JEWISH PEOPLE
AT BEIT HATFUTSOT

Dear educator,

Engaging our students with Jewish heroes is a great way to get them to think about bigger questions regarding their lives and the world around them. Heroes are our role models, a source of inspiration for developing character traits that foster personal growth and encourage positive action in the world. Here are our goals as we launch this exploration of Jewish heroes with our children:

Relevancy: Discussing heroes and trailblazers is a great way to talk to children about what matters to them, why it matters, and how to do something about it. The issues the heroes in this book confront—treating others kindly, calling out injustice, expressing our identity as individuals and as Jews—are just as relevant now in the work of Ruth Bader Ginsburg as they were when Isaiah spoke out in ancient Israel. They will help students notice how they encounter these same issues in their personal lives as well.

Personal Connection: When we think of heroes, we often imagine superheroes or military heroes—strong and athletic. But heroes come from all walks of life. They were not born heroes, rather they became heroes through the choices they made to use their strengths and overcome their vulnerabilities. The Jewish heroes in this course reflect the diversity of Jewish identity in the realms of faith, religion, and culture—from Steven Spielberg, with a cultural and historical outlook on Jewish identity, to King David, who according to tradition wrote songs of praise to God. And it is through these diverse, all-too-human heroes that students can recognize their own varied relationships to Jewish life and their ability to carve their own future in that identity.

Empowerment: Heroes like Natan Sharansky or Henrietta Szold changed the world: through Sharansky's activism, Russian Jews were able to leave the Soviet Union; and Szold helped countless children and adults in need of medical care. They inspire and challenge us to be our best selves and to make the world a better place. This can seem daunting to our students. Don't be afraid to challenge them—they don't need to save thousands of lives in order to have an impact; instead they can think and act in small ways to make a difference in their home, at school, and in their community.

At the Museum of the Jewish People at Beit Hatfutsot in Tel Aviv, we have an exhibition called "Heroes—Trailblazers of the Jewish People," dedicated to more than 140 heroes from around the Jewish world. These heroes inspire us to challenge ourselves, to draw on our strengths, and to improve ourselves and the world. We have found teaching children about Jewish values and history through heroes to be a profoundly rewarding experience. We hope you do, too.

Assaf Gamzou
Director of Museum Education
Museum of the Jewish People at Beit Hatfutsot
Tel Aviv, Israel
www.bh.org.il

Introduction

About *The Hero in Me*

The Hero in Me introduces five character traits—courage, kindness, creativity, curiosity, and fairness—from a Jewish perspective, guiding students to connect with their heritage on a deeper level. The series consists of five 8-page booklets, each centered on a single trait. Students will study Jewish heroes who have embodied these traits and consider how they, too, can incorporate the traits into their daily lives. By studying heroes who range from biblical to modern, young to old, famous to lesser-known, students will discover how they can be heroic in a variety of ways.

Each booklet contains:

- An introductory page that describes the character trait covered in the booklet.
- Biographical sketches of two Jewish heroes whose lives exemplify the trait. One is a historical figure, the other modern. Their stories are presented interactively to help readers understand the heroes as relatable role models.
- Activities and discussion questions to encourage critical thinking about each hero.
- "From the Text," a feature that connects the trait with traditional Jewish sources.
- A profile of a heroic young person who embodies the trait today.
- "Listen Up," a feature that explores musical selections, especially classic and contemporary popular songs, that express the trait.
- Other activities such as personality quizzes and art projects to help students determine how they relate to the trait.
- An at-home activity that offers opportunities to hone the trait outside of class.

About This Teacher's Guide

Each chapter of this guide covers one student booklet and comprises an introduction and a guide for conducting three lessons. Each lesson will take roughly 35–50 minutes to conduct.

The lessons can be spread out through the year or used consecutively over approximately fifteen classes. They can also be used during family programs, as parents and students may enjoy exploring their Jewish traits as a family.

Each lesson can be completed in a single class period, aside from activities that need follow-up. If, for example, lesson 2 of a unit includes an activity with follow-up, you can assign the activity in lesson 2 and follow up at the beginning of lesson 3.

There are also optional "Taking It Further" activities that allow students to dive deeper into each heroic trait. You can use these as time and resources allow.

The introduction to each chapter includes the following:

- **Enduring Understandings:** Key ideas that students will take away from the unit. These understandings can help students build lifelong Jewish values.
- **Heroes Overview:** Additional background information about the life and achievements of the historical heroes profiled in the booklet. You can use these during a discussion to expand on the lives of the heroes.

- **Word(s) to Know:** Definitions of the one or two Hebrew words used in the student booklet.
- **Customize:** Brief descriptions of the three lesson plans in the chapter, and suggestions for choosing the elements that work best for your needs.

Each chapter of the book includes the following:

- **Essential Question:** A question at the beginning of the lesson that engages students in thinking about a central theme.
- **Learning Objectives:** What students will accomplish.
- **Getting Started:** Quick ways to prepare and energize your students for the activities to come.
- **Lesson Activities:** Activities that elaborate on the text in the booklet using art, music, skits, discussion prompts, and more, and suggestions for ways to apply the ideas to students' personal lives.
- **It's a Wrap!:** A brief activity to review the main themes of the lesson.
- **Taking It Further:** Enrichment activities to extend learning as time and resources allow.
- **Bringing the Character Trait Home:** An activity that students can complete with family members, friends, and/or mentors outside of class. Each activity includes "Follow-Up" questions for the beginning of the next lesson.

The student booklets are designed to be flexible. The character traits can be taught in any order, and students can easily bring the booklets home to share the material with their families.

If you wish to dedicate more time to a lesson, the "Taking It Further" activities provide many ways to do so, and the questions and activities are designed to generate thoughtful conversations. Allowing extra time for these conversations can help students deepen their personal connections to Jewish values.

In addition to the materials found in this guide, there are many resources available to you on the Behrman House website, www.behrmanhouse.com/hero. The webpage is organized by chapter, and each link within the page includes a brief description. Throughout this guide, you will see prompts to visit this site. You can use the online materials in class as time and resources allow, or you can guide students to use them at home.

Experiential and Project-Based Learning

Many lessons in this guide include "Experiential Learning" and "Project-Based Learning" activities, which provide additional opportunities to explore the themes of the lessons.

- **Experiential Learning** takes students beyond classroom reading, writing, and discussion, allowing them to apply what they've learned via hands-on activities. Students can further engage with the material via art, music, skits, and more.
- **Project-Based Learning** allows you to lead student-driven projects with real-world applications. Students will forge deeper connections to Judaism by pursuing their own interests in a way that has a tangible effect on the world around them. For example, a Project-Based Learning activity centered on social action might prompt students to think of social justice causes they care about. Then, using the Jewish values they've explored in the lesson, they could brainstorm ways to support those causes: donating to charity, raising awareness through posters, creating a proposal for a new organization or club, and more.

Being Inclusive

The activities in this guide employ a range of learning modalities, ensuring that a diverse group of learners will succeed. In general, by employing a variety of teaching approaches, you will be able to reach the widest range of children with different learning styles. You may also find that some students need additional support. Be mindful of students who seem to be struggling with the material; you may need to modify certain activities for them.

It can be helpful to find out from parents or from a school administrator if any accommodations are being made in a child's other school experiences. The following suggestions can help ensure success for all students:

- After going over a passage from the student booklet, ask questions to clarify points of potential misunderstanding, and invite students to do the same. Look for ways to connect the information to students' lives.
- Allow students to be flexible in creative tasks. When necessary, adapt those tasks to suit students' skills and strengths. For example, if a student is too shy to participate in a skit, you could encourage that student to watch the skit and share observations at the end.
- Invite students to paraphrase and summarize what they've learned.

Remember, teaching and learning are among the greatest of all Jewish values. As you help your students develop their own courage, kindness, creativity, curiosity, and fairness, you will become their hero, too.

CHAPTER 1

COURAGE

Enduring Understandings

- It sometimes takes courage to take even small steps.
- We *can* overcome challenges that can stop us from doing the things we want or need to do.
- Being courageous might mean overcoming fear, even in the face of danger, so we can help our families, our communities, and the world.
- Stories of courageous Jewish heroes can inspire us to develop courage in ourselves.

Courage Heroes Overview

Queen Esther is the heroine of the Book of Esther, a biblical story set in ancient Persia. The book follows her fate after King Ahasuerus makes her his queen, favoring her over all the other young Persian women brought to the palace and paraded before him. Mordecai, Esther's uncle, advises her to keep her Jewish identity a secret. But things change when Haman, one of the king's officials, develops a plan to kill all the Jews in the Persian Empire. Mordecai calls upon Queen Esther to use her connection to the king to foil this evil plan. At first, Esther is afraid to take any action, knowing she might lose her life if she approaches the king without permission. But finally, she bravely invites the king and Haman to a feast. There, she reveals her Jewish identity and pleads with Ahasuerus to save her nation. Ahasuerus allows the Jews to defend themselves and orders that Haman be hanged. We celebrate how the Jewish nation was saved on the holiday of Purim.

Natan Sharansky is an activist, author, and former Israeli politician who advocates for human rights around the world. Sharansky began standing up for others when he lived in the former Soviet Union in the 1970s. He was born in the Ukraine in 1948 and had applied to leave the Soviet Union for Israel in 1973. But the Soviet government turned down his request. Sharansky became a leader in the Soviet Jewry movement, fighting for the right of Russian Jews to leave. As a result, the Soviet authorities arrested him in 1977 and falsely accused him of being a spy. They sentenced him to thirteen years in prison. He continued to stand up for his values there, holding hunger strikes to protest the harsh treatment of prisoners. Meanwhile, his wife led a worldwide campaign to pressure the Soviets to release him. Her efforts finally paid off when the Soviets freed Sharansky in 1986, allowing him to go to Israel. Sharansky continued to help Russian Jews there by starting a political party to represent them. Today, he writes and speaks about important issues facing democracies around the world.

What Is Courage?

Courage is the strength to persist in the face of fear, pain, uncertainty, temptation, and other challenges.

Words to Know

***gibor*:** someone strong and courageous; a hero (the Hebrew root of *gibor* means "to overcome")

***ometz leiv*:** courage; the strength to overcome fear

Customize

This chapter includes three lesson plans for *The Hero in Me: Courage*:

1. What does Jewish tradition teach us about courage? (page 3)
2. What inspires heroes to act bravely? (page 5)
3. How can we take a stand for what we believe in? (page 7)

You can use all three complete lessons or choose your favorite ideas from each and craft your own lesson plan. Here are some ideas for customizing the material in this chapter:

- **For a focus on Jewish tradition**, do these activities: "Getting Started: Models of Courage" (page 3), "From the Text" (page 3), "Word-Wise" (page 3), "Courage Hero: Queen Esther" (page 5), and "Project-Based Learning: Modern *Megillot*" (page 6).
- **If you only have time for one lesson about *The Hero in Me: Courage***, do these activities: "Getting Started: Models of Courage" (page 3), "What Is Courage?" (page 3), "Courage Hero: Natan Sharansky" (page 5), "What's Your Courage Style?" (page 7), and "It's a Wrap!" (lesson 3, page 8).

Lesson 1: What Does Jewish Tradition Teach Us About Courage?

Learning Objectives: Students will:

- Develop a concept of courage based on Jewish values.
- Explore how *anyone* can be brave.

Materials

- pencils
- markers
- paper
- magazines
- glue
- scissors

LESSON ACTIVITIES

Getting Started: Models of Courage (5 minutes)

Write the word *courage* on the wall on a whiteboard, a large sticky note, or another medium. Ask: Who would you give a medal to for being the most courageous person of the year? Then write the answers on the wall. Answers may include specific names or whole categories of people, like firefighters. Answers may also include public figures or people the students know personally. Discuss their answers and the reasons for their choices, writing their reasons on the wall too.

What Is Courage? (5 minutes)

Ask what students notice about the cartoons of Queen Esther and Natan Sharansky on page 1 of the booklet. *(they have serious expressions; Esther is wearing a crown; Sharansky is opening his mouth to speak)* Based on the pictures, how might they have shown courage? *(Esther used her position as queen to help others; Sharansky spoke out for what's right)* What, if anything, do you know about their lives? You may wish to supplement their answers with biographical information from the chapter introduction (page 1).

From the Text (5–10 minutes)

Ask students to complete the activity at the top of page 3 of the booklet in pairs or small groups. After they discuss the questions, ask volunteers to give their interpretation of what the rabbis meant by mastering yourself. *(not saying mean things; overcoming your shyness by introducing yourself to a new person)* Ask: How did Sharansky model this definition of strength? *(by not letting his captors humiliate him; by focusing on his deepest values)*

Word-Wise (5–10 minutes)

Have students create definition flash cards for *gibor* and *ometz leiv*. They should write the word or phrase on the front, then on the back write the definition and sketch a related image. Direct students to trade a card with a friend, and then ask volunteers to present their friend's card to the class. Ask: Based on the image, how does your friend's idea of courage differ from your own? How is it similar? Now that you've seen another perspective on courage, has your own perspective changed?

Committees on Courage (15 minutes)

Organize students into small groups. Guide the groups to each create a magazine cover entitled "Courage Hero of the Year," based on the concepts of the booklet. If they wish, they can use the "courageous person of the year" suggestions from the beginning of the lesson. Provide them with paper, glue, scissors, and markers. Direct each group to develop a concept for their cover that includes the names and images of the heroes, as well as visuals related to their courageous actions. Ask one volunteer per group to present their cover to the class.

It's a Wrap! (5 minutes)

Ask: Based on what you learned, what might be a definition of courage informed by Jewish values? *(standing up for what you believe in; protecting the vulnerable; doing what's right even when it's hard; persevering in the face of obstacles)* Have a few volunteers share situations in which they showed courage.

TAKING IT FURTHER

Courage Memorials

Tell students that they'll have an opportunity to honor some of the heroes they've discussed. Divide students into small groups, then have each group choose a hero or group of heroes from the "Getting Started" activity. Share pictures of a few memorials with a range of styles and meanings (e.g., the Lincoln Memorial, the Vietnam Veterans Memorial, the Washington Monument), and instruct them to design their own memorials in honor of the heroes. Ask: Based on the pictures you've seen, how might you honor the heroes in a unique, beautiful way? Have students sketch the designs, then hang them around the classroom.

Lesson 2: What Inspires Heroes to Act Bravely?

Learning Objectives: Students will:

- Understand how Queen Esther and Natan Sharansky showed courage in the face of exceptional challenges.
- Explore how heroes choose to act bravely at key points in their lives.
- Consider what it takes for people to be courageous in difficult or even dangerous situations.

LESSON ACTIVITIES

Getting Started: To Be or Not to Be Brave? (5–10 minutes)

Discuss with students a time when they had to make a hard decision. Ask: What action did you take to improve the situation? Remind them that many people experience turning points in their lives when they must decide whether to act courageously, and when they choose a courageous path, often they become leaders.

Courage Hero: Natan Sharansky (10–15 minutes)

What Would You Do?

- Direct students to create a double-sided work page by making two columns on a piece of paper. Have them write "What Happened to the Hero" at the top of the left column and "How the Hero Felt and Acted" at the top of the right column.
- Ask: What happened to Natan Sharansky that was beyond his control? Direct students to look at his bio on page 2 of the booklet for answers. Have students list those things in the left column.
- Ask: What actions did Natan Sharansky take in response to those events? How did he feel? Direct students to list those things in the right column.
- Have students pair up and debate the "WWYD?" questions on page 3 of the booklet. One student will argue for "yes," one for "no." Ask: What are the pros and cons of doing what Sharansky did? Are there different ways of showing courage in this situation? Then ask one pair to share their pros and cons with the class.
- Read aloud the quote on the same page. Ask: What point does Sharansky make about how you feel about a difficult situation? *(a positive outlook can transform a negative situation; we're in charge of our thoughts and feelings—nobody can decide them for us; we can't always decide what happens to us, but we can decide how to act)* Direct students to add items to the double-sided work page about how Sharansky felt and acted.

Courage Hero: Queen Esther (5–10 minutes)

- Give students some background information on Queen Esther based on her mini-bio on page 1 of this guide. Have students read Queen Esther's text conversations on pages 4–5 of the booklet to each other in small groups. Direct them to add her actions and feelings, based on the text, to the double-sided work pages.

- Provide groups with pencils and papers to write their own text messages, based on other moments from the *megillah*. Encourage students to think about how Queen Esther's courage might shape those conversations. For example, Esther could be texting the Jews about how she saved them from Haman. Invite volunteers to share their texts with the class.

Courage in Common (10–15 minutes)

- Direct students to complete the "Courage in Common" activity on page 5 of the booklet. Ask: What challenges did each person face? *(prejudice from powerful people around them; dangerous situations; uncertainty over their futures)* How do you think they overcame their fears? *(by focusing on their deepest values; by reminding themselves how important it is to stand up for others)*
- Lead a debate over which hero was braver. Split the group into two teams: Team Sharansky and Team Esther. Alternate between teams to let students share their points of view. Encourage students to use everything they've learned to shape their arguments.

It's a Wrap! (5 minutes)

Ask: What is one courageous action you have taken that is similar—even a little—to one of Queen Esther's or Natan Sharansky's? When deciding how to take action, which people, concepts, and memories gave you the courage to take that action?

TAKING IT FURTHER

Experiential Learning: All's Well That Ends Well

Discuss with the class what happened to Queen Esther. Then go to www.behrmanhouse.com/hero and watch the video about Natan Sharansky. Ask the class to describe brave actions that Sharansky and his wife took during his years in prison. Invite students to imagine that Queen Esther and Natan Sharansky are asked to be on a panel to speak about the trait of courage. Choose two volunteers to represent them. Then direct students to ask the volunteers questions about courage and the brave actions they took.

Project-Based Learning: Modern *Megillot*

We read the story of Queen Esther from a *megillah*, a scroll, on the holiday of Purim. Divide students into small groups and provide them with drawing paper, markers, and crayons. Assign each group a modern Jewish hero, and provide information about that hero, available at www.behrmanhouse.com/hero. Instruct each group to write and illustrate a modern-day *megillah* that describes that person's heroic actions. Invite students to present their scrolls to the class, teaching them about new heroes.

Lesson 3: How Can We Take a Stand for What We Believe In?

Learning Objectives: Students will:

- Learn how anyone, even young people, can become courage role models.
- Discover how courage can manifest in many ways, big and small.
- Explore ways that students can practice courage in their daily lives.

LESSON ACTIVITIES

Getting Started: Taking a Stand (5–10 minutes)

Ask: How can music make us feel brave? *(when we identify with a song's message, we're inspired to act; an upbeat song gives us energy; songs help us identify other people who believe in what we believe in)* Go to www.behrmanhouse.com/hero and play several songs of courage to the class, as mentioned in the "Listen Up" activity on page 8 of the booklet. Invite students to stand up and move in time with the music. Then discuss how the music made them feel and how it affected their movements. Ask: What do you think the songwriters were trying to communicate? As a class, develop a courage playlist of five songs or tunes that might give people strength.

Courage in Action: Sam Verstandig (5–10 minutes)

- Divide the class into small groups, and instruct them to read the section about Sam Verstandig on page 6 of the booklet together and come up with the answer to: What problem did Verstandig solve? What about his action was courageous? What did he have to overcome? *(Verstandig saw a bully scaring another kid, so he intervened; he was courageous because the bully might have turned on him; he overcame his fear by realizing that it was important to him, and to his values, to take action)*
- Direct the groups to review the "Work Your Courage Muscles" questions on page 6 of the booklet. Then have each student write an action plan for overcoming their fear that includes the specific fear, the action they want to take, obstacles they might face, and a support network of people and other resources to help them achieve their goal. Invite volunteers to share their ideas.

What's Your Courage Style? (10–15 minutes)

Instruct students to complete the quiz on page 7 of the booklet independently. Then read aloud the descriptions of the different kinds of courage personalities. Select one volunteer for each courage style to improvise a skit for the class showing that style in action. Present the volunteers with a scenario that requires courage (standing up for a friend, confronting a peer about a mistake, confiding in a parent), and have them act out what they'd do in that situation, based on their courage styles. You may wish to involve additional students in the skit to fulfill other roles (for example, a friend, a parent, or a bully).

Bringing Courage Home (5 minutes)

- Review the interview activity on page 8 of the booklet. Read aloud the following quote from Pirkei Avot: "Who is wise? He who learns from everyone." Ask: Who in your life can you learn about courage from, even if you don't know them well? Invite a few volunteers to describe friends or family members who have shown courage. Encourage students to interview a family member about a time when that person was courageous and to prepare to share what they learned at the beginning of the next lesson.

- **Follow-Up:** Invite volunteers to share what they learned in their interviews. Ask: What surprised you about what you learned? How might you use this story of courage to guide your own actions?

Hero Toolkit (5–10 minutes)

Sharansky read the *Book of Psalms*, a gift from his wife Avital, many times during his imprisonment. In many of the psalms, King David describes challenges that he faced and the strength he needed to confront them. Ask students to draw objects that inspire them to be brave. Then ask them to add captions that explain how the items help them feel courageous.

It's a Wrap! (5 minutes)

Courage is like a muscle: the more we use it, the stronger it gets. Instruct students to write, on sticky notes, one small step they can take every day to exercise their courage muscles. Then have students stick their notes on a classroom wall. Encourage students to walk around the room to read these courage tips. Ask: What's a tip that surprised you? Which tip (not your own) might you try? Consider asking them to stand next to the note not their own that they found most helpful. See which tips are the most helpful, and discuss with the class.

TAKING IT FURTHER

The Courage to Take Action

Direct students to watch the interview of Natan Sharansky at www.behrmanhouse.com/hero to learn about actions he has taken to help others after he was freed. Read the following quote aloud:

> "In dictatorships you need courage to fight evil; in the
> free world you need courage to see evil."
> —Natan Sharansky

Discuss the quote and Sharansky's actions with the class. Ask: Why is it hard to see evil in the free world? *(evil takes many forms, big and small; sometimes things appear okay, but there's more going on beneath the surface; in the age of social media, when opinions and false information are freely disseminated, it can be hard to learn the truth)* Then direct students to write down either a small problem they've noticed (such as in school, in a club, or on a team) or a social justice issue they care about. Have them list three small steps they can take to address it. Ask volunteers to share their ideas.

CHAPTER 2

KINDNESS

Enduring Understandings

- We can draw on Jewish tradition to help us be kind in our daily lives.
- We can support others by identifying their needs and then using our time, possessions, money, and—most importantly—our empathy to address those needs.
- Acts of kindness, both small and large, can have far-reaching and long-lasting results.

Kindness Heroes Overview

Henrietta Szold (pronounced "zold") was born in Baltimore, Maryland in 1860. As Jewish immigration to the United States grew in the late nineteenth century, Szold started a night school to help immigrants learn English and civics. In the early twentieth century, she began to help Jews settling in Palestine in the hopes of building a Jewish state. She founded the American Zionist Medical Unit and the women's Zionist organization now known as Hadassah. Hadassah focused on providing up-to-date medical care, education, and social services in Palestine. In the 1930s, under Szold's direction, Hadassah sponsored Youth Aliyah, saving thousands of young people from the Nazis by settling them in Palestine. Today, Hadassah remains an active Jewish organization, and Hadassah Hospital in Jerusalem is one of Israel's leading medical centers.

Doña Gracia Nasi is famous for using her wealth to help other Jewish people. She was born Beatrice de Luna in Portugal in 1510. Her family was forced to convert to Christianity but secretly continued practicing Judaism as best they could. Beatrice married a wealthy merchant, and when he died, she inherited much of his fortune. Although officially converted as a "New Christian," she was not safe in Portugal. She and her family fled to Istanbul, where under the Ottoman Empire they could live openly as Jews. Beatrice changed her name to Doña Gracia Nasi, and she began helping other Jews and forced converts. She built synagogues, schools, and hospitals. For conversos—Spanish and Portuguese Jews forced to convert to Christianity, who often tried to continue practicing Judaism—she had Hebrew books translated and published in Spanish. She also rented land to rebuild a settlement in Tiberias where Jews fleeing Europe could settle safely. Sadly, Doña Gracia Nasi died before she could move to Tiberias herself.

What Is Kindness?

Kindness is behavior that shows care for other people, the desire to help them, or the desire to make them happy.

Word to Know

chesed: an action that will help others, rather than oneself

Customize

This chapter includes three lesson plans for *The Hero in Me: Kindness*:

1 What does Jewish tradition teach us about kindness? (page 11)

2 How do kindness heroes change the world? (page 13)

3 How can we apply the lessons of kindness heroes to our own lives? (page 15)

You can use all three complete lessons or choose your favorite ideas from each and craft your own lesson plan. Here are some ideas for customizing the material in this chapter:

- **For a focus on social action**, do these activities: "Getting Started: Acts of Kindness" (page 11), "Kindness Hero: Henrietta Szold" (page 13), "Community Kindness" (page 12), and "Kindness in Action: Sara Blau" (page 15).
- **For a focus on Jewish tradition**, do these activities: "Word-Wise" (page 11), "Getting Started: Kindness versus Charity" (page 15), "Kindness Hero: Doña Gracia Nasi" (page 13), "From the Text" (page 14), and either "Kindness Comics" (page 12) or "'Tzitzit' Bracelets" (page 16).
- **If you only have time for one lesson about *The Hero in Me: Kindness***, do these activities: "Getting Started: Acts of Kindness" (page 11), "What Is Kindness?" (page 11), "Kindness Hero: Henrietta Szold" (13), "How Do You Show Kindness?" (page 15), and "It's a Wrap!" (lesson 3, page 16).

Lesson 1: What Does Jewish Tradition Teach Us About Kindness?

Learning Objectives: Students will:

- Develop an understanding of kindness informed by Jewish values.
- Explore ways to be kind based on Jewish teachings and tradition.

Materials

- drawing paper
- index cards
- pencils
- crayons or markers
- string

LESSON ACTIVITIES

Getting Started: Acts of Kindness (5 minutes)

Write the word *kindness* on a whiteboard, a large sticky note, or another medium. Ask students: What are some actions that show kindness? Discuss their answers and how each one shows kindness. List their ideas under the word *kindness*.

What Is Kindness? (5–10 minutes)

Divide students into small groups to review the introduction on page 1 of the booklet. Direct students to circle words or phrases that demonstrate kindness. *(care; attention; supporting; connected; saw their needs; worked; help; taking actions)* Invite volunteers—at least one per group—to share some of the words and phrases they found. Then ask: How does kindness go beyond "being nice"? Encourage students to use some of those kindness words in their answers. *(being nice can just be on the surface; kindness can mean taking action to help others; being nice is good, but sometimes it covers up deeper problems)*

Word-Wise (5–10 minutes)

Tell students that this activity will reflect how acts of kindness build on one another, connect people, and mend the world. Arrange students in a circle, and give each one a flash card with two hole punches in it, one on each edge. Ask a volunteer to write #1 and an act of *chesed* on their card, then pass it to the person on their left. Have the next student read that card, write #2 on their own card, and write an act of *chesed* related to the one on card #1. Go around the circle until everyone has written on their cards. Then have them connect the flash cards with string in numerical order and hang the "chain of *chesed*" around the classroom. Remind students that even the smallest acts of kindness build community.

Experiential Learning: Kindness Charades (10–15 minutes)

Write a few of these kind acts on small pieces of paper. Have students take turns selecting and acting out these acts while the rest of the class guesses what they are.

It's a Wrap! (5 minutes)

Ask: Based on what you learned, how is kindness part of Jewish life? *(Jewish organizations like Hadassah promote a message of kindness; Jewish heroes use their faith as inspiration to help others)* How can acts of kindness strengthen Jewish communities? *(acts of kindness help Jews feel more connected; when we support each other, we can face challenges together)*

TAKING IT FURTHER

Kindness Comics

Remind students that Jews have a long tradition of kindness heroes going back to the Bible. As a class, identify ways in which famous Bible heroes were kind. *(in Genesis, Abraham and Sarah are kind by opening their tent and providing hospitality to visitors; Rebekah is kind by giving water to a man and his camels when they were traveling, even though she doesn't know him; in the Book of Ruth, Ruth is kind to Naomi by staying with her and bringing her food)* Provide printouts from www.behrmanhouse.com/hero on the relevant Bible stories to use as resources. Then have students each choose one hero and create a one- or two-page comic with panels, illustrations, and speech bubbles illustrating the hero's act of kindness. Exhibit the finished comics in the classroom.

Community Kindness

Remind students that a person does not need to be wealthy like Doña Gracia Nasi to donate money. Many Jewish organizations, including Hadassah, raise money from the larger Jewish community. Both large and small donations help these organizations carry out their mission of kindness. Go to www.behrmanhouse.com/hero and information about Jewish *chesed* organizations such as Hadassah, JCFS, HIAS, and American Jewish World Service. Invite students to work in groups to choose one *chesed* organization and create a poster about its past and present acts of kindness and why it is a good place to donate money. Then hold a Kindness Panel where students can bring in tzedakah and groups can present their posters to the class. As a class, make a plan to donate the tzedakah to one or more of the organizations.

Lesson 2: How Do Kindness Heroes Change the World?

Learning Objectives: Students will:

- Learn how Henrietta Szold and Doña Gracia Nasi were models of how to use our Jewish background and values to build kindness traits.
- Consider the impact of one person's kind actions on others.

LESSON ACTIVITIES

Getting Started: Effects of Kindness (5–10 minutes)

Have students think about a time when someone was kind to them or they were kind to another person. Ask them to describe what happened, if anything special inspired them to act, and how they felt afterward. Take notes on the board, a large sticky note, or another medium about the effects of these kind actions.

Comparing Kindness: Venn Diagram

Direct students to create a Venn diagram by drawing two large overlapping circles on a sheet of paper. Have students label one circle "Henrietta Szold" and the other "Doña Gracia Nasi." Students will fill in this diagram as they read about these kindness heroes.

Kindness Hero: Henrietta Szold (5–10 minutes)

- Ask students to underline as many kind actions as they can find in Henrietta Szold's profile on page 2 of the booklet. Have students add those actions to Szold's circle in the diagram.
- Tell students to imagine they are volunteers for the American Zionist Medical Unit. Ask: How would volunteering be challenging? How would it be rewarding? Have students record challenges on sticky notes of one color and rewards on sticky notes of another color. Stick these notes around the room, and allow students to circulate to read all the ideas.
- Ask students to go over the "Think About It" discussion questions on page 3 of the booklet in pairs or small groups. Then invite volunteers to share ways they can look for opportunities for kindness.

Kindness Hero: Doña Gracia Nasi (5–10 minutes)

- Ask students to underline as many kind actions as they can find in Doña Gracia Nasi's profile on page 4 of the booklet. Have students add those actions to Doña Gracia Nasi's circle in the diagram.
- Have students compare the two kindness heroes and write similar acts of kindness in the overlapping center of their Venn diagrams. Ask: What do these similarities tell us about kind people and their actions? *(kind people are generous; kind acts can help large groups of people; care for Israel and the Jewish people can inspire other Jewish people to perform acts of* chesed*)*
- Doña Gracia Nasi used money for acts of *chesed*. Ask: How can people who do not have much money also be generous? *(they can give of what resources they do have, such as their time or their expertise)* Invite students to brainstorm ways they can use Doña Gracia Nasi's generosity as a model, including ways that do not involve money.

Meet Aaron Feuerstein (10–15 minutes)

- Ask students to read the feature about Aaron Feuerstein on page 5 of the booklet and discuss: Why might it have been hard for Feuerstein to keep paying his workers after the fire? *(he had lost a lot, including a big part of his business)* Why do you think he chose to pay them? *(he cared about them; he did not want them to lose a lot, too)* What can his actions teach us about kindness? *(even when things are tough, we can think of others as well as ourselves)*
- Direct students to write a letter from Aaron Feuerstein to his workers, expressing thanks for the opportunity to be kind. Suggest that students consider Feuerstein's feelings about the fire, his workers, and the factory reopening.

From the Text (10–15 minutes)

- Have students stand straight up, with their feet firmly planted on the floor. Point out how their legs support their body so that it feels stable. Then ask a volunteer to read the Pirkei Avot quote on page 5 of the booklet. As a class, define what it means that the world "stands" on acts of kindness. *(these actions hold up the world, like people's legs when they stand; without acts of kindness, people would feel less supported and stable)*
- Ask: How do the kind acts of Feuerstein, Doña Gracia Nasi, and Szold relate to the quote? *(these kind acts contributed to the health, happiness, and success of people in need; by being kind, the three heroes supported their communities)*
- Point out the image of the world with the hands holding it up, at the bottom of page 5 of the booklet. Ask: What does it make you think of? *(working together; diversity; community; interdependence)* Divide students into small groups, and provide each group with poster paper, crayons, and markers. Direct them to create posters about the world "standing on" acts of kindness, using the image and the Pirkei Avot quote as inspiration. *(images might include: people in confident poses, physically supporting each other; people holding hands; people holding up a globe, making a declaration of kindness in a speech bubble)* Hang the posters in the classroom.

It's a Wrap! (5 minutes)

Ask: How can you make an impact—now or in the future—that is even a little bit like Henrietta Szold's, Doña Gracia Nasi's, or Aaron Feuerstein's? Invite volunteers to share situations from their own lives that would be improved with a little kindness.

TAKING IT FURTHER

Experiential Learning: Acting Out Kindness

Tell students that they'll have a chance to compare the heroic actions of Henrietta Szold and Doña Gracia Nasi in this activity. Divide students into small groups, and ask them to imagine that Szold and Doña Gracia Nasi are discussing their heroic actions. Ask: What questions would they ask each other? Where would they find common ground, and where do their experiences diverge? Direct the groups to create short skits that include Szold, Doña Gracia Nasi, and a discussion moderator. If there are more than three students in a group, the non-actors should write most of the script. Encourage students to draft questions for the moderator while leaving room for improvisation. Invite students to present their skits to the class. Then lead a discussion comparing the impact of Henrietta Szold and Doña Gracia Nasi.

Lesson 3: How Can We Apply the Lessons of Kindness Heroes to Our Own Lives?

Learning Objectives: Students will:

- Learn how young people, like Sara Blau, can become kindness role models and help others do the same.
- Explore how we can use our unique skills and interests to perform kind acts.

LESSON ACTIVITIES

Getting Started: Kindness versus Charity (5–10 minutes)

Write this statement from the Talmud on the board: "Acts of kindness are superior to charity." Then divide the class into two groups: one that supports the quote, and one that doesn't. Lead a debate about which is superior, acts of kindness or acts of charity. Alternate between groups so that students have a chance to present their views. *(possible pro-kindness answers: charity can be performed only with money, while acts of kindness can be performed both with actions and with money; charity is given to the poor, while acts of kindness are performed both for the poor and for the rich) (possible pro-charity answers: charity enables people to become more independent; people can choose what to do with the charity they receive, whereas specific acts of kindness may be less flexible)*

Kindness in Action: Sara Blau (5–10 minutes)

- Invite groups to look at the photo and caption on page 6 of the booklet. Ask how it shows the impact of Blau's kindness. *(Sarah has helped thousands of kids around the world play sports with the correct equipment; the photo shows kids using some of their new equipment)*
- Ask: What led Sara Blau to identify this global issue? Why was she so passionate about it? *(she loves sports; she was motivated to help others based on a shared passion)* Direct students to write three things they're passionate about. Ask: How might one or more of these things lead to a kind act? *(love of animals can lead to volunteering at an animal shelter; love of writing can lead to writing poems and stories for friends)*

Listen Up (10–15 minutes)

Divide students into small groups and assign each of them a song about kindness from www.behrmanhouse.com/hero. Then review the discussion questions on page 6 of the booklet as a class. Ask: How do these unique songs inspire unique sounds and movements? *(upbeat songs inspire snapping, stomping, and desk-tapping; slow songs encourage humming and slow clapping)*

How Do You Show Kindness? (5 minutes)

Instruct students to complete the quiz on page 7 of the booklet independently. Then read the descriptions of the various ways to show kindness, asking students to raise their hands when their way is read. Create small groups based on each way of showing kindness. Have each group brainstorm more situations where they can show kindness in this way, and invite one student per group to share those ideas.

Work Your Kindness Muscles (5–10 minutes)

Complete the activity on page 8 of the booklet as a class. Then guide students to toss the ball to one another for a second round. Each time someone catches it, ask them to describe one way that being kind was tough for them *or* one thing that helped them be kind during the week. Make sure that every student gets a turn.

Bringing Kindness Home (5–10 minutes)

- Review the activity on page 8 of the booklet. As a class, brainstorm things that each student might want to put on their slips of paper, based on their work about kindness in the booklet. Ask students to be ready to share their experiences with their families at the beginning of the next lesson.
- **Follow-Up:** Invite volunteers to share what they and their families discussed in response to the questions on page 8 of the booklet. Ask: How did it feel to practice kindness at home? What did your family think? Would you do this activity again? Why or why not?

It's a Wrap! (5 minutes)

Remind students that they have many chances to exercise their kindness "muscles." Ask: How do kind acts on a big scale (like founding Hadassah, building synagogues, and founding Game Changers) relate to kind acts on a smaller scale? *(both involve caring about the welfare of others and sometimes putting them first; big acts of kindness often start with small ones; I may not have the resources to do something grand, but I can choose kindness every day)*

TAKING IT FURTHER

"Tzitzit" Bracelets

Tell students that it is sometimes difficult for each of us to remember to exercise our kindness muscles. For that reason, the Torah describes a visual reminder for people to wear: the fringes, or tzitzit, on the corners of a tallit are intended to remind the person wearing it to follow the *mitzvot* (commandments) in the Torah, including acting kindly. Ask students to inspect the tzitzit on a tallit, and show them the video at www.behrmanhouse.com/hero. Then invite students to create their own visual reminder to do their chosen act of kindness. It could be using yarn, string, or paper strips to make "tzitzit" bracelets. It could be a rubber band worn on the wrist, or a pin, or any of their own ideas.

CHAPTER 3

CREATIVITY

Enduring Understandings

- Jewish tradition and history provide many examples of creativity, including visual art, storytelling, and problem-solving.
- When we appreciate the creative achievements of others, we can build creativity in ourselves.
- The world can inspire us to be creative when we keep our minds and hearts open.

Creativity Heroes Overview

Steven Spielberg was born in 1946 in Cincinnati, Ohio, and his family later moved to Arizona and then California. As a Jewish child, he often felt like an outsider and sometimes faced overt anti-Semitism. He was keenly aware of the Holocaust, both from stories about family members who had been killed and from survivors he knew. Spielberg began directing films as a teenager and dropped out of college to work in television. He became a successful director and producer at a young age, and he has made many hit films and won five Oscars throughout his career. Several of his films deal directly or indirectly with Jewish topics. Cartoonish Nazi villains and the biblical Ark of the Covenant play important parts in *Indiana Jones and the Raiders of the Lost Ark*; the animated children's movie *An American Tail* focuses on a European Jewish mouse immigrant to the United States; *Schindler's List* centers on the Holocaust; and *Munich* depicts the massacre of Israeli athletes at the 1972 Olympics and the aftermath of the massacre. Spielberg used the profits from *Schindler's List* to start the Shoah Foundation, which has collected more than fifty thousand recordings of survivors telling their stories.

King David was the second king of Israel, ruling around 1000 BCE. David's story is told in the biblical Book of Samuel. The biblical Book of Psalms is also traditionally attributed to King David, and scholars have tried to connect various psalms to different points in his life. David was the youngest son of Jesse and a descendant of Ruth, from the Book of Ruth, and he began life as a shepherd. As a young man, he was called to the court of King Saul and became a war hero for his part in fighting the Philistines, including defeating their champion Goliath. Though David was connected to Saul's family by marriage and friendship, the king became jealous of David's success and persecuted him, but he escaped. After the deaths of Saul and his sons, David was anointed king of Israel. David had a successful reign, including defeating the Philistines, but a turbulent family life. He had multiple wives and even arranged for the husband of the beautiful Bathsheba to be killed in battle so he could marry her. Later, several of his older sons went to war with each other and with him. After David's death, his younger son Solomon became the next king. Solomon was renowned both for his wisdom and for building the First Temple in Jerusalem.

What Is Creativity?

Creativity is the ability to see things in new ways, find new forms of expression, and make new things.

Word to Know

***y'tziratiyut*:** creativity

Customize

This chapter includes three lesson plans for *The Hero in Me: Creativity*:

1 What does Jewish tradition teach us about creativity? (page 19)

2 How do creativity heroes express their ideas? (page 21)

3 How can we express our creativity using our unique skills and interests? (page 23)

You can use all three complete lessons or choose your favorite ideas from each and craft your own lesson plan. Here are some ideas for customizing the material in this chapter:

- **For a focus on modern arts**, do these activities: "What Is Creativity?" (page 19), "Creativity Hero: Steven Spielberg" (page 21), "Meet Michael Twitty" (page 22), "Getting Started: Creative Movement" (page 23), and "Experiential Learning: Creating a Museum Exhibit" (page 20).
- **For a focus on traditional Jewish texts**, do these activities: "Getting Started: The Root of Creativity" (page 19), "Word-Wise" (page 19), "Creativity Hero: King David" (page 22), "From the Text" (page 22), and "Ancient Meets Modern in Psalm 150" (page 22).
- **If you only have time for one lesson about *The Hero in Me: Creativity***, do these activities: "Getting Started: The Root of Creativity" (page 19), "What Is Creativity?" (page 19), "Creativity Hero: King David" (page 22), "What Creative Type Are You?" (page 23), and "It's a Wrap!" (lesson 3, page 24).

Lesson 1: What Does Jewish Tradition Teach Us About Creativity?

Learning Objectives: Students will:

- Develop an understanding of creativity based on Jewish values.
- Explore how people can be creative using their unique interests and strengths.

Materials

- writing and drawing paper
- index cards
- pencils
- crayons or markers
- paint
- glue
- scissors

LESSON ACTIVITIES

Getting Started: The Root of Creativity (5–10 minutes)

Write the word *creativity* on a whiteboard, a large sticky note, or another medium. Ask: What action word can you see in this word? *(create)* Point out that creating is an important part of Jewish life. The Torah describes God as creating the world in six days and resting on the seventh. Likewise, Judaism encourages people to work creatively during the week and rest on Shabbat, the seventh day. Ask students to brainstorm some other examples of creativity in the Torah.

What Is Creativity? (5 minutes)

Direct students to look at the cartoons of King David and Steven Spielberg on page 1 of the booklet. Ask: What do you notice about them? How do you think they express(ed) their creativity? *(King David is playing a harp—maybe he composed songs; Spielberg is holding an Oscar—he expressed himself through filmmaking)* Then guide students to look at the text on the page. Ask students to brainstorm other forms of creativity. *(inventing something; painting a picture; acting in a play; designing a garden; writing a story)*

Word-Wise (5 minutes)

Post the word *y'tziratiyut* on the wall on a whiteboard, a large sticky note, or another medium and tell students what it means. Provide them with paper, markers, and crayons. Tell them that calligraphy is part of Jewish creativity, and encourage them to write the word in a creative way—in cursive or in block letters, using images that resemble the words, or working in color, for example. Encourage students to draw a scene or design around the word if they'd like to. Post the drawings around the classroom to remind students that *y'tziratiyut* takes many forms.

Hidur Mitzvah (15–20 minutes)

Tell students that there is a Jewish concept called *hidur mitzvah*—literally "beautifying the mitzvah"—adding beauty to important religious objects and activities. This concept has inspired the creation of beautiful, ornate ritual objects such as candlesticks, Kiddush cups, challah covers, spice boxes, *etrog* boxes, etc. Show students a few of these objects or pictures of them. Then, as a class, quickly review a variety of both ethical and ritual *mitzvot*, such as giving tzedakah, *tza'ar ba'alei chayim* (taking care not to needlessly harm animals), lighting Shabbat candles, waving a *lulav* on Sukkot, and treating others fairly. You might provide an initial list and then ask for additional suggestions from volunteers. Have students work alone or in small groups to choose one mitzvah and sketch or draft a way to add beauty to it. Ask: How can you add beauty to the mitzvah through a song, story, or other medium? If students wish to design a physical object, what materials will bring the design to life? Suggest that students designing objects use symbols to reflect the *mitzvot*. For example, a challah cover might have a peace sign on it, because Shabbat is a peaceful time. Invite students to present their completed designs or drafts to the class. Ask: What inspired your designs? What surprised you about the creative process?

It's a Wrap! (5 minutes)

Ask: Based on what you learned, how can creativity enrich Jewish life? *(creativity allows people to bring their own ideas and talents to their Jewish life; it can help people find new meaning in old traditions and rituals)*

TAKING IT FURTHER

Experiential Learning: Creating a Museum Exhibit

Tell students that they will be creating a museum-style exhibit about Jewish creators. Provide students with a list of prominent Jewish creators: artist Marc Chagall, composer and singer Debbie Friedman, scientist Albert Einstein, writer Judy Blume, writer and artist Maurice Sendak, Superman creators Jerry Siegel and Joe Shuster, actor Gal Gadot, and pop star Matisyahu. Ask students to work individually or in small groups to choose one creator or set of creators. Direct students to visit www.behrmanhouse.com/hero to research the creator(s) of their choice. Students should consider these questions: How was the person creative? How can I highlight their creativity in a poster or other kind of exhibit? Then have students create a poster, diorama, or other exhibit about the creator. Display the finished products in a class creativity museum. Invite families and other classes to visit the museum.

Lesson 2: How Do Creativity Heroes Express Their Ideas?

Learning Objectives: Students will:

- Learn how Steven Spielberg, King David, and Michael Twitty expressed creativity.
- Explore how Jewish values can help people pursue their passions.

LESSON ACTIVITIES

Getting Started: Creative Types (5–10 minutes)

Play a creativity game: Ask students to stand in a circle and throw a ball to another player. As students catch the ball, they must name a creative person and briefly tell why that person is creative. Remind students that creative people include musicians, filmmakers, cooks, writers, inventors, and problem-solvers. Make sure everyone gets a turn.

Inspirations for Creativity: Flow Chart

Direct students to create a simple flow chart by drawing one box, then an arrow leading to a second box. Have students label the chart "Steven Spielberg." Direct students to draw another, identical chart labeled "King David." Then have students label the first box in each chart "Inspiration" and the second box "Achievements." Students will fill in these charts as they read.

Creativity Hero: Steven Spielberg (5–10 minutes)

- Ask students if they already know anything about Steven Spielberg. Ask: What are some of his creative achievements? Then guide them to name more achievements based on the profile on page 2 of the booklet. Have students write the achievements in their own words in Spielberg's flow chart. *(he made movies and created the Shoah Foundation)*
- Invite a volunteer to read the quote from Steven Spielberg on page 3 of the booklet. Ask: Based on the creative achievements you just named, how does this quote relate to his work? *(he wanted to tell stories that connected people)* Have students add this inspiration to their chart.

What Would You Do? (10–15 minutes)

Divide students into three groups, and assign each group a diary entry from page 2 or 3 of the booklet. Tell the groups to discuss how Spielberg used his creativity to solve problems. Direct students to add these as "inspirations" and "achievements" to their charts.

- For the *Jaws* group: Tell students that Spielberg had another idea: filming some scenes underwater, as if from the shark's point of view. Ask: How else could Spielberg have addressed the problem using creativity?
- For the *E.T.* group: Point out the photo of E.T. on page 2. Ask: How did the filmmakers use their creativity to render the alien? *(they had to imagine what an alien would look like; they gave E.T. some familiar physical features so that viewers would identify with him on a deeper level)*
- For the Holocaust survivors group: Ask: How did Spielberg's creativity build community? *(he gave survivors the chance to share their stories; when we learn about other people's struggles, we empathize more)*

Creativity Hero: King David (5–10 minutes)

Ask students if they know who King David was. Refer them to the profile on page 4 of the booklet if they need help. Then ask them to name something creative that he did. *(he wrote the Book of Psalms; he used creative problem-solving to fight Goliath)* Have students add these as "inspirations" and "achievements" to King David's flow chart.

From the Text (5–10 minutes)

- Direct students to look at the psalm on page 4 of the booklet. Ask: How do images in the psalm connect to King David's life? *(his experience as a shepherd may have inspired him to write about God as a shepherd)* Have students add these to their charts.
- Go to www.behrmanhouse.com/hero and play the psalm sung to a common tune. Ask: How do the music and images in this video show creativity? *(they match the words but express the ideas in new ways; there are many other melodies and images that the artists could have used)*

Meet Michael Twitty (10–15 minutes)

- Have students work in small groups to read the profile of Michael Twitty on page 5. Then ask students to brainstorm foods that have a connection to Jewish tradition. *(holiday foods like challah and matzah; Israeli foods like falafel and hummus)*
- Have students refer to the list to plan their own dish combining Jewish food culture and another tradition that has meaning for them. Ask students to write a description or create an illustration of their dish. Invite students to present their dish to the class, including a brief description of its origin.

Creativity in Common (5–10 minutes)

Have students work in pairs to read and complete the dialogue on page 5 of the booklet. Then ask them to act it out, with one partner as King David and one as Twitty. If you have an odd number of students, include in one group an interviewer who asks King David and Michael Twitty about their creative passions. Encourage students to improvise additional dialogue and follow-up questions. Invite volunteers to perform their skits for the class.

It's a Wrap! (5 minutes)

Ask: How are the creative achievements of Steven Spielberg, King David, and Michael Twitty alike? *(they all stem from the heroes' passions and values; they all build community by illuminating our common experiences)* How might you apply these ideas to your life?

TAKING IT FURTHER

Ancient Meets Modern in Psalm 150

Provide students with the text of Psalm 150 in English, and read it aloud. You can find the text at www.behrmanhouse.com/hero. Point out the words that suggest creative musical ways to praise God. Then go to the website and show videos of several modern musical settings of the psalm. Once students have reviewed the videos, ask students to vote on their favorite version of the song, based on how well the melody fits the lyrics. Ask them to discuss why they made the choice they did.

Lesson 3: How Can We Express Our Creativity Using Our Unique Skills and Interests?

Learning Objectives: Students will:

- Learn how young people, like Sela Boord, can be creativity role models in a Jewish context.
- Identify with one or more ways in which people are creative.
- Explore ways that they can build their creativity trait in their daily lives using Jewish values.

LESSON ACTIVITIES

Getting Started: Creative Movement (5–10 minutes)

Tell students that the Israeli music star Idan Raichel became famous for his creativity in blending music styles from around the world, including the Middle East and Ethiopia. Then tell students that they will have a chance to improvise creative movements to go with one of Raichel's most popular songs. Go to www.behrmanhouse.com/hero and play the hit song "Boee" for the class. Divide students into small groups, and have groups take turns leading the class in creating dance or hand movements to go with the music.

Creativity in Action: Sela Boord (5–10 minutes)

- Ask a volunteer to read aloud the profile of Sela Boord on page 6 of the booklet. Ask: What inspired Sela to be a clown? *(she wanted to help sick kids laugh; she wanted to use her passion for performing arts to connect with others)*
- Ask: How might expressing creativity in this way be challenging for Boord? *(she needs to have a lot of things ready to try so she can connect to different patients; she has to put herself out there, without always knowing how people will react)* Point out that expressing creativity often involves practice and hard work, as well as inspiration. Students will have an opportunity to explore this in the next activity.

Work Your Creativity Muscles (10–15 minutes)

- Divide students into pairs or small groups to do the activity on page 6 of the booklet. Then ask them how it felt to try so many versions of their jokes. *(it was fun to try new things; it felt good to improve the joke; it was hard to think of new ways to tell the joke)*
- Invite students to film the funniest version of their joke. Compile the videos to create a virtual show to share with students' families. If possible, and with permission, offer to share the show with a local children's hospital or pediatric unit.

What Creative Type Are You? (5–10 minutes)

- Instruct students to complete the quiz on page 7 of the booklet independently. Then read the descriptions of the various ways to show creativity.
- Invite one volunteer per creative type to act out one of the scenarios in the quiz. Encourage them to take it a step further by improvising what they would do, based on their creative type. Then

ask them: How did it feel to collaborate with other creative types in order to solve the problem? Ask the whole class: How else could people respond to the scenario?

Think About It (5–10 minutes)

- Direct students to complete the activity on page 8 of the booklet. To help students think about what inspires them, allow them to review their flow charts about experiences that inspired Steven Spielberg and King David. Encourage students to consider their senses as well as inspiring places, people, or feelings.
- Direct students to create a flow chart of "inspirations" and "achievements" based on what they've written and discussed. Ask students to consider how creativity has already shaped their lives. If students feel stuck, encourage them to create a flow chart of "inspirations" and "goals" instead. Ask: What do you *want* to achieve based on the things that inspire you? Invite volunteers to share their work with the class.

Bringing Creativity Home (5 minutes)

- Talk about the activity on page 8 of the booklet, and encourage students to do it that week. Ask them to be prepared to share their experiences at the beginning of the next class.
- **Follow-Up:** Ask students whether they would try any of these new uses again. Then ask them to name situations where this kind of creative thinking could be useful. *(if you forget something on a trip; if you're locked out of your house; if you run out of something you need)*

It's a Wrap! (5 minutes)

Ask: What have you learned about yourself by considering several modes of creativity? How do you hope to express your creativity in your daily life? Encourage students to give specific situations from their lives that might allow for creativity.

TAKING IT FURTHER

Express Your Creativity

Remind students that many creative people find inspiration in connecting with others. For example, Steven Spielberg wanted to connect with people's feelings through storytelling on film and to preserve the stories of Holocaust survivors. King David wrote poems to feel closer to God. Sela Boord uses humor to help young people cope with being in the hospital. Invite students to choose one of their sources of inspiration and use it to create something to help or connect with others. It could be a work of art, a song, a card, a story, a photograph, a video, a website, a game, an object, or something else. Invite students to share their creation with the class and briefly explain their goal and inspiration, as well as any challenges they faced in bringing their idea to life.

CHAPTER 4

CURIOSITY

Enduring Understandings

- We are capable of pursuing the subjects of our curiosity, even in the face of exceptional challenges.
- Curiosity can lead to innovative ways of understanding the world, as well as to practical inventions.
- Jewish tradition teaches us that we can deepen our curiosity by being open to everyone, by examining our own perspectives, and by having new experiences.

Curiosity Heroes Overview

Moses ben Maimon, popularly known as **Maimonides**, was born in Córdoba, Spain, around 1135. When his family's ability to live freely as Jews was threatened, they relocated several times to other parts of the Muslim world, finally ending up in Fostat, Egypt, near Cairo. There, Maimonides became the official leader of the Jewish community, as well as a renowned physician serving the sultan and the royal family. His curiosity led him to investigate and write about a wide range of subjects, including Jewish law (the *Mishneh Torah*), philosophy (the *Guide for the Perplexed*), medicine (he wrote ten known works on medicine), the calendar, prophecy, faith, and the afterlife. In addition, his statements of what constitutes true faith have become an integral part of Jewish belief. Christians and Muslims, as well as Jews, continue to find meaning in his work even today. Rambam—an acronym of the first Hebrew letters of **R**abbi **M**oses **b**en **M**aimon (with added vowels)—died in 1204 and was buried in Tiberias, now in Israel. His curiosity made him such a prolific writer and influential thinker that an inscription on his tomb even compared him to the original Moses from the Torah, stating: "From Moses to Moses, there was no one like Moses."

In the late 1990s, **Amit Goffer** was badly injured in an ATV accident near his home in northern Israel. After many months of feeling helpless, Goffer decided to use his skills as an inventor and entrepreneur to reclaim his life. He didn't understand why wheelchairs had changed so little for hundreds of years. His questions—along with support from Israel's Technion Institute—led him to invent the ReWalk, an exoskeleton-like device that allowed paraplegics to walk again. Goffer himself couldn't use the ReWalk, yet the curiosity that stemmed from his personal trauma evolved into a humanitarian effort and added profound meaning to his life. The company he developed to manufacture this device helped its users and also fostered Israeli-Palestinian cooperation in Israel.

What Is Curiosity?

Curiosity means questioning the world and seeking out new information, ideas, and experiences.

Words to Know

sakranut: curiosity

tzedakah: literally, justice or righteousness; often refers to acts that are considered moral obligations in Jewish tradition, including charity (money given to someone in need)

Customize

This chapter includes three lesson plans for *The Hero in Me: Curiosity*:

1. What does Jewish tradition teach us about curiosity? (page 27)
2. How does a hero's curiosity lead to innovation? (page 29)
3. How can we use our curiosity to make a difference in our communities? (page 31)

You can use all three complete lessons or choose your favorite ideas from each and craft your own lesson plan. Here are some ideas for customizing the material in this chapter:

- **For a focus on Jewish tradition**, do these activities: "Getting Started: Curious Questions" (page 27), "Word-Wise" (page 27), "Curiosity Hero: Maimonides" (page 30), "From the Text" (page 31), and "Get Curious about 'Yigdal'" (page 32).
- **If you only have time for one lesson about *The Hero in Me: Curiosity***, do these activities: "Getting Started: Curious Questions" (page 27), "What Is Curiosity?" (page 27), "Curiosity Hero: Maimonides" (page 30), "Think About It" (page 32), and "It's a Wrap!" (lesson 3, page 32).

Lesson 1: What Does Jewish Tradition Teach Us About Curiosity?

Learning Objectives: Students will:

- Develop a concept of curiosity based on Jewish values.
- Identify and discuss ways that each of us can explore our curiosity.

Materials

- drawing paper
- index cards
- pencils
- crayons or markers

LESSON ACTIVITIES

Getting Started: Curious Questions (5 minutes)

Write the word *curiosity* on a whiteboard, a large sticky note, or another medium. Point out that curious people ask a lot of questions. Ask: When do you most often have questions? *(when I'm confused; when I want to know more about something; in school; when I meet new people)* When you have questions, what helps you learn more? *(asking those questions directly; being open to what people have to say; doing research; examining my beliefs and experiences)* List their ideas on the board, a piece of butcher paper, a large sticky note, or other medium.

What Is Curiosity? (5 minutes)

Direct students to look at the cartoons on page 1 of the booklet. Ask students if they know anything about Goffer or Maimonides, and direct them to look at the text if they need help. Ask: How did these people act on their curiosity? *(Amit Goffer invented a machine to help paralytics; Maimonides developed new explanations of religion, medicine, and philosophy when he didn't understand them as well as he wanted to)* How do you act on your curiosity in ways that are similar or different?

Word-Wise (5–10 minutes)

Provide students with paper, markers, and crayons. Direct students to write either *sakranut* or *tzedakah* on the paper, then draw an image or images that relate to that word. Ask: What does *curiosity* mean to you? What acts of tzedakah have you done or would you like to do? How might *tzedakah* relate to curiosity? Hang the drawings on the walls, and invite students to share what inspired them.

Project-Based Learning: Curiouser and Curiouser (15 minutes)

Ask: What makes people curious? *(learning something new; being in a new place; meeting someone new; facing a new problem)* What do people do when they are curious that helps them learn? *(ask questions; try to answer questions; try new things; find new information)* Ask students to work in small groups to create a one-page comic showing the process of curiosity—encountering something new, asking questions, and gathering information. Invite groups to share their comics with the class.

It's a Wrap! (5 minutes)

Ask: How did Maimonides and Amit Goffer express curiosity from a Jewish perspective? *(Maimonides learned and wrote about Jewish texts and ideas; Goffer invented something to benefit others, not just himself; Maimonides teaches that we should get to know the world we live in, because that will help us appreciate God more)* How can you express curiosity from a Jewish perspective? *(by asking questions about Jewish texts or traditions; by treating Jewish people from history and our own lives as our teachers)*

TAKING IT FURTHER

Questioning the Passover Seder

Curiosity plays a part in many areas of Jewish life, and asking questions is particularly important during the Passover seder. In addition to the Four Questions in the haggadah, the rabbis in the Talmud would even use tricks to get children to ask questions. For example, one rabbi set his entire table upside down "so that the children should see and ask." Have students work with a partner to come up with ways to inspire more questions at the seder. For example, you could serve dessert first, eat in a different part of the house from usual, wear special clothes, have interesting decorations, do a show, or tell jokes. Make sure students understand that the purpose of the task is to inspire questions, not generate answers. Ask pairs to illustrate or write a brief description of at least one of their ideas to share with the class. Then invite other students to ask questions about the scene. If appropriate, suggest that students try some of their ideas at either a school or home seder this year.

Lesson 2: How Does a Hero's Curiosity Lead to Innovation?

Learning Objectives: Students will:

- Consider what it takes for curiosity to lead to innovation and accomplishment, even in the face of complex problems and situations.
- Identify positive effects of acting on our curiosity, such as creating new technology and ways of thinking.

LESSON ACTIVITIES

Getting Started: Inventing Curiosity (5 minutes)

Ask students what inventions they use in this learning space. *(pens; pencils; notebooks; whiteboard; art supplies; computers; desks)* List their ideas on the wall. Then ask students to explain what need each invention fulfills. *(capturing ideas; creating art; accessing the Internet; sitting comfortably)* Point out that an inventor's curiosity and questions started the process that created these things and addressed these needs.

Curiosity Hero: Amit Goffer (10–15 minutes)

- Divide students into small groups to go over Amit Goffer's profile on page 2 of the booklet. Ask: How did Goffer use curiosity to transform a terrible situation? *(he treated that situation as an opportunity to change the world; he focused on other people's needs and suffering, not just his own; he saw a problem and explored solutions)* Ask students to each write down a challenge they face. Then ask them to share those challenges with their groups. Direct the groups to brainstorm ways to address these challenges using curiosity. Invite volunteers to share their ideas with the class. Ask: How did sharing a problem with the group make you feel? How has your perspective on that problem changed?
- Direct students to look at the photo of Claire Lomas on page 2 of the booklet. Ask: How do you think she felt in that moment? Then tell students to imagine that they need to use a ReWalk as well. Direct them to write thank-you notes to Amit Goffer describing how his innovation has transformed their lives. Ask: How might you also help people using your curiosity?

Work Your Curiosity Muscles (5–10 minutes)

- Go over the activity on page 3 of the booklet, and invite students to brainstorm situations they could choose besides the ones listed there. *(cooking or eating a new food; talking to someone new at school; exploring a new place)* Remind students that they should get permission for activities outside of school from an adult in their family. Tell students they'll have a chance to share their experiences at the beginning of the next lesson.
- **Follow-Up**: Divide students into pairs or small groups to discuss what they learned. Then ask: After having this new experience, is there anything you'd like to do differently?

Curiosity Hero: Maimonides (5–10 minutes)

- Point out the subheading for Maimonides's profile on page 4 of the booklet: "Philosopher. Rabbi. Doctor." Ask: What do you think Maimonides was curious about? *(the essential nature of being Jewish; Jewish traditions; medicine; physical health)* Encourage students to look at his profile for clues.
- Have students work in pairs to read the social media chat aloud and complete the chat in their booklet. As a class, discuss whether students agree or disagree with Maimonides and the tzedakah-giver. Ask: Is it always better to give someone a job than to give them money? What other kinds of tzedakah might people give? *(goods; skill training)* Are there situations where certain kinds of tzedakah might be better than others, or are some kinds always better?

Supercurious (10–15 minutes)

- Go over the activity on page 5 of the booklet. To help students think of tools to help a curiosity superhero, ask what Goffer and Maimonides might have used to help with their inventions and ideas. *(books; websites; building tools; astronomy supplies; medicines)*
- Have students complete their superheroes and discuss the questions in small groups. Invite students to share what tools they gave their superheroes and why, as well as any additional tools they themselves can use to understand the world.
- Tell students to imagine that Amit Goffer and Maimonides are superheroes. Ask: Who would be more powerful? Divide the class into two teams, one for each superhero. Lead a debate in which students describe the superheroes' unique tools, costumes, abilities, and strategies. Encourage students to use everything they've learned about their superhero to argue why he would be more powerful.

It's a Wrap! (5 minutes)

Ask: Based on what you've learned, how do you want to hone your curiosity superpower? What issues do you hope to address using your powers of curiosity?

TAKING IT FURTHER

Experiential Learning: From ReWalk to UPnRIDE

Go to www.behrmanhouse.com/hero and show students the video about Amit Goffer's new invention, the UPnRIDE. Discuss the many questions that Goffer had to ask and answer in the course of inventing it. Then have students work in groups to design their own inventions to help people with mobility or other physical challenges. Ask groups to think about the issues they need to overcome (for example, staircases, broken sidewalks, or buses) and to list questions they'd have to answer to create their inventions. Have each group create a poster introducing their invention and identifying key questions and challenges. Then have an inventors' panel where groups can take turns presenting their posters, with time for additional questions from the class.

Lesson 3: How Can We Use Our Curiosity to Make a Difference in Our Communities?

Learning Objectives: Students will:

- Learn how young people, like Tamar Beer, can be curiosity role models.
- Discuss the many ways in which people express or practice their curiosity and which ways students connect with.

LESSON ACTIVITIES

Getting Started: A Curiosity Activity (5–10 minutes)

Ask students to name a favorite activity, such as playing sports, cooking, or making videos. Ask: How did you first learn about this activity? How do you learn new things about it or improve your skills with it? What would you still like to know about it? Once everyone has had a turn to share, ask: How could your curiosity help you do that activity better or enjoy it more?

Curiosity in Action: Tamar Beer (5–10 minutes)

- To help students understand Beer's focus on women's learning, explain that in some very traditional Orthodox communities, men and women do many things separately, and women sometimes have fewer opportunities to study Jewish texts. Beer was trying to solve this problem.
- Have students work in small groups to read the profile of Tamar Beer on page 6 of the booklet and name things that she was curious about. *(learning about Jewish tradition; why there was no program for Jewish learning for women in her neighborhood; how to help women take part in Jewish learning)*
- Ask students to name a problem they see in their community. *(neglected public spaces; homelessness; discriminatory behavior)* Ask: How can your curiosity help you address this problem, as Beer did?

From the Text (5–10 minutes)

- Read the quotation from Pirkei Avot on page 6 of the booklet aloud. Ask: How can engaging with others help us build our curiosity? *(it gives us hints of things we then want to know more about; it shows us clues of where we can learn more)*
- Go over the activity on pages 6–7 of the booklet. If students are struggling to come up with questions, suggest starters such as: "How did you learn to . . . ?"; "What is the best way to . . . ?"; "How can I . . . ?"
- Divide students into pairs or small groups to go over the discussion questions on the bottom of page 7 of the booklet. Then invite volunteers to each share one question that they wrote. Try to collect at least one question for each picture. Then have a class discussion about the challenges and rewards of learning from other people. *(challenges: understanding a perspective that's different from mine; being respectful when I disagree with someone) (rewards: broadening my*

perspective; considering other hobbies and approaches I might try; becoming kinder and more open-minded by listening to everyone)

Think About It (10–15 minutes)

- Have students write their question on page 8 of the booklet and make their research plan in class. Host a curiosity "podcast" where students can take turns interviewing each other about their questions, research plans, and how this topic has sparked their curiosity. Then ask them to research their question outside of class. Tell them they'll have a chance to share what they've learned at the beginning of the next lesson.
- **Follow-Up:** Invite a few volunteers to share what they've discovered. Ask: Whom did you ask for help and why? Did the answer to your question surprise you?

Bringing Curiosity Home (5–10 minutes)

- Go over the at-home activity on page 8 of the booklet. Tell students they'll have a chance to share what they've learned at the beginning of the next lesson.
- **Follow-Up:** Ask students to report what problem they tried to solve at home. Ask: How did you find out more about the problem? What did you learn? What solution did you try? Did it work? Why might it have worked or not worked? Point out that not all inventions work the first time. Curious inventors keep asking questions to improve their work.

It's a Wrap! (5 minutes)

Ask: Name a topic you are curious about. What ideas do the activities in this lesson give you about how you could explore this topic, now or in the future?

TAKING IT FURTHER

Project-Based Learning: Get Curious about "Yigdal"

Tamar Beer helped girls and women get involved in learning from Jewish texts. Tell students that they will have a chance to learn from a Jewish text, too. Ask students to look in a siddur at the hymn called "Yigdal." (The Hebrew words and English translation, as well as a traditionally sung version of the hymn, are also available at www.behrmanhouse.com/hero.) Tell students that this song, traditionally sung at the end of Friday night services, is based on the Thirteen Principles of Faith written by Maimonides—the ideas that Maimonides thought were most important for Jews to believe. Read the English translation as a class, and display or pass out a list of shortened versions of the principles, out of order. (One translation can be found at www.behrmanhouse.com/hero.) Have students work in groups to choose one principle and think more deeply about it. Ask: Why might Maimonides find this idea so important? What questions do you have about it? Ask groups to use their questions and ideas to prepare their own songs or poems expressing their curiosity about the principle. Invite the groups to present their songs or poems to the class.

CHAPTER 5

FAIRNESS

Enduring Understandings

- Fairness involves treating all people in a way that shows respect for their humanity and not favoring some over others for illegitimate reasons.
- We can build our fairness trait by respecting other people's perspectives and putting ourselves in their shoes.
- We can speak out for fairness even when it is difficult or unpopular.
- Jewish tradition emphasizes the importance of fairness by encouraging respect for all, speaking out against injustice, and taking action to ensure that others are treated fairly.

Fairness Heroes Overview

Ruth Bader Ginsburg was born in Brooklyn, New York, in 1933. Her father was an immigrant from Russia, and her mother's parents had come to the United States from Poland. The family led an active Jewish life, and Jewish values informed Ginsburg's lifelong pursuit of justice. Although neither of her parents was able to go to college, Ginsburg attended Cornell University, then began law school at Harvard before transferring to Columbia. As a Jew, a woman, and a mother, Ginsburg experienced frequent discrimination in her early life and career. Yet she persisted and became a lawyer, then a law professor, and then a judge. In her work as co-director of the ACLU's Women's Rights Project and as co-author of a book on gender discrimination, she advocated for women's rights. She argued six cases before the Supreme Court—winning five of them—before being nominated to the court herself in 1993. As a member of the Supreme Court, Ginsburg has continued to make her voice heard, both through questioning in oral arguments and through forcefully written opinions and dissents, as well as enjoying strong relationships with other members of the court from across the political spectrum.

The biblical prophet **Isaiah**, son of Amoz, lived in Jerusalem at the time of the First Temple. During this turbulent time, Judea was threatened by regional powers such as Assyria, Egypt, and Babylonia. Despite these outside pressures, Isaiah emphasized a clear, consistent moral message. He criticized injustice, especially disregard of the poor and vulnerable by the rich and powerful, and demanded that people change their ways. In political and military matters, he urged trust in God rather than in outside powers. He even explained the threats Israel faced from God's displeasure with the people's behavior. Although little is known about the end of Isaiah's life, some Jewish traditions suggest that he became a martyr because of his strong advocacy of monotheism.

What Is Fairness?

Fairness is treating all people with respect, in ways that show we value them and recognize their humanity. It means not giving more favorable treatment to some people over others for no legitimate reason.

Word to Know

tzedek: justice, or fairness in action

Customize

This chapter includes three lesson plans for *The Hero in Me: Fairness*:

1. What does Jewish tradition teach us about fairness? (page 35)
2. How do fairness heroes stand up for people? (page 37)
3. How can we build our own fairness trait? (page 39)

You can use all three complete lessons or choose your favorite ideas from each and craft your own lesson plan. Here are some ideas for customizing the material in this chapter:

- **For a focus on present-day activism**, do these activities: "Getting Started: Facing (Un)Fairness" (page 39), "Fairness Hero: Ruth Bader Ginsburg" (page 37), "Fairness in Action: Jacob Revels" (page 39), "Work Your Fairness Muscles" (page 39), and "Diving into *Tzedek*" (page 36).
- **If you only have time for one lesson about *The Hero in Me: Fairness***, do these activities: "Getting Started: Fair or Unfair?" (page 35), "What Is Fairness?" (page 35), "Fairness Hero: Isaiah" (page 38), "Work Your Fairness Muscles" (page 39), and "It's a Wrap!" (lesson 3, page 40).

Lesson 1: What Does Jewish Tradition Teach Us About Fairness?

Learning Objectives: Students will:

- Develop an understanding of fairness rooted in Jewish values.
- Explore how each of us can build our fairness trait by acting and speaking out against injustice.

Materials

- drawing paper
- large paper for posters
- pencils
- crayons or markers

LESSON ACTIVITIES

Getting Started: Fair or Unfair? (5 minutes)

Ask students to brainstorm arrangements, relationships, and situations in their lives that they consider fair. Invite a few volunteers to share. Then ask the class: What makes them fair? Do other students agree that these situations are fair? Why or why not? What could make them even better? Then ask students to brainstorm unfair arrangements, relationships, and situations from their lives. Ask: What makes them unfair? Do other students agree that these situations are unfair? Why would people choose to act unfairly? What are the consequences of the unfairness? Tell students they'll have a chance to explore these questions further in the lesson.

What Is Fairness? (5 minutes)

- Point out the cartoons on page 1 of the booklet. Ask students if they know anything about these figures. Then ask: How did they fight for fairness? Encourage students to look at the text for clues.
- Tell students that Ruth Bader Ginsburg and Isaiah chose to be fair despite exceptional challenges. Ask: Why might it be hard to be fair? *(I can't always resolve unfair situations on my own; if I don't have all the facts, I won't always know what's fair; being brave is vital to bringing more fairness into the world, and sometimes it's hard to be brave)* How can you respond to unfair situations? *(educating myself on the issue; collaborating with others to address it; raising awareness)*
- Ask students to identify groups of people whom each fairness hero helped. *(Ruth Bader Ginsburg helped women; Isaiah helped widows and orphans)* Guide students to understand why these groups needed advocates. Help them see that throughout history, women have not had equal rights at work or in their families. When men had more rights and usually earned the family's money, women and children whose husband or father had died often became poor. Tell students they'll have a chance to use this information in the next activity.

Word-Wise (5 minutes)

Provide students with paper, markers, and crayons. Direct them to write the word *tzedek* and draw a related image, based on the discussion of Ginsburg and Isaiah. Encourage students to draw Ginsburg and/or Isaiah acting fairly. Have students compare their images with a partner and discuss how each shows fairness. Encourage students to consider how their image differs from their partner's. Ask:

What do these differences teach you about fairness? *(fairness can take many forms; it's important to consider unfair situations from many angles)* Hang the drawings up around the classroom.

Prophecy Posters (15 minutes)

Isaiah spoke out for the disadvantaged. Ask: Who is treated unfairly today? *(racial minorities; LGBTQ people; immigrants; poor people; religious minorities; disabled people)* Ask: What unfair treatment do these people face? *(violence; lack of access to social resources such as medical care; rights that are limited by law)* Why might people treat these groups unfairly? *(because they cannot see these people's humanity; because ignorance and hatred can lead to destructive ideas about other groups)* What changes can we make to improve their situations? *(we can be empathetic and kind; we can raise awareness about social issues; we can support laws and other social initiatives to protect rights for all)* Then ask students to create a poster urging a specific change to make the world fairer. Remind students that prophets and advocates use strong, direct language to express their values, as well as convincing details—such as showing people who are suffering from injustice—to make their point. Display the posters in the classroom as a reminder to treat all people fairly.

It's a Wrap! (5 minutes)

Ask: What is one act of fairness that you have observed or done in a Jewish context (e.g., at the synagogue, in Hebrew school, on a holiday)? How does that action fit with what you have learned about fairness?

TAKING IT FURTHER

Diving into *Tzedek*

Go to www.behrmanhouse.com/hero and watch the video in which Rabbi Danya Ruttenberg compares *chesed* (a voluntary act of giving based on personal caring), tzedakah (money or services given to people in need), and *tzedek* (creating meaningful change to make the world more just). Have students identify acts of *tzedek* shown or discussed in the video. As a class or in small groups, discuss the ways in which these actions promote fairness. Then have students list at least three things that would be different if our world were based on *tzedek*. Ask: How can we work to make these ideas a reality? If there is time, ask students to illustrate one of the changes they envision. (For example, if they suggested that people should have equal access to housing, they might draw a diverse neighborhood.)

Lesson 2: How Do Fairness Heroes Stand Up for People?

Learning Objectives: Students will:

- Explore how heroes combat injustice, even when they face opposition or danger.
- Identify both large and small manifestations of fairness in the world.

LESSON ACTIVITIES

Getting Started: The Job of a Judge (5–10 minutes)

Ask students what they know about judges. Encourage students to name any famous court cases they can think of. *(answers will vary: Roe v. Wade; Citizens United v. Federal Election Commission; Brown v. Board of Education)* Ask: Why is fairness so important for the role of a judge? *(people deserve to receive unbiased treatment; when judges focus on fairness, they make balanced and educated decisions)* As a class, identify other jobs where fairness is important and explain why. List answers on the board.

Finding Fairness: Venn Diagram

Direct students to create a Venn diagram by drawing two large overlapping circles on a sheet of paper. Have students label one circle "Ruth Bader Ginsburg" and the other "Isaiah." Students will fill in this diagram as they read.

Fairness Hero: Ruth Bader Ginsburg (10–15 minutes)

Ask: What prepared Ruth Bader Ginsburg to serve on the Supreme Court, the highest court in the United States? Direct students to review Ginsburg's profile on page 2 of the booklet for answers. *(she was a lawyer before becoming a judge, so she already had courtroom experience)* Have students write acts of fairness in Ginsburg's circle in the Venn diagram.

What Would You Do?

- Before students begin the activity on page 2 of the booklet, review the Virginia Military Academy (VMI) case with them. Have them identify the original situation, why the woman filed the lawsuit, and the school's position.
- Divide students into groups to complete the dialogue on pages 2–3 of the booklet. Invite one or two groups to perform their dialogues for the class. Encourage them to improvise dialogue that fits with the themes of the script. Direct students to add facts to their Venn diagrams.

What Did Justice Ginsburg Think?

- Have the groups discuss why VMI was excluding women. *(people thought women could not handle the demands of VMI; people thought women would have needs the school could not address)* Point out that people may once have considered this situation fair. Direct students to add to their Venn diagrams based on the discussion.
- Ask: How do people change their ideas of what is fair? *(by listening to new perspectives; by challenging social norms to make the world fairer for everyone)*

Fairness Hero: Isaiah (10–15 minutes)

Have students work in the same groups to read Isaiah's profile on page 4 of the booklet. Ask what Isaiah did and why. *(he criticized the rich for ignoring the poor and vulnerable; he wanted people to do what was fair)* Have students add their answers to their diagrams.

From the Text

- Invite volunteers to put each quotation on page 4 of the booklet in their own words. *(God could have said, "Why are you celebrating?" or "I hate the way you celebrate my holidays.")*
- Direct the groups to act out the comic panel on page 4. Encourage them to speak expressively. Then have the groups go over the discussion questions, and invite a few volunteers to share their thoughts with the class.
- Direct students to write acts of fairness that are shared by both Ginsburg and Isaiah in the middle of their Venn diagrams. Point out that Ginsburg and Isaiah have vastly different backgrounds and experiences, yet their actions have a lot in common. Invite volunteers to share some of the similarities they found.

Remembering Chaney, Goodman, and Schwerner (10–15 minutes)

- Ask: In what ways were African Americans treated unfairly in the early 1960s? What did James Chaney, Andrew Goodman, and Michael Schwerner decide to do about it? Guide students to look at the text on page 5 of the booklet for answers.
- Reread the quote from Rita Schwerner. As a class, discuss how people today can continue to build on the murdered men's legacy. *(make sure all Americans have equal voting rights; donate to organizations devoted to social justice)*

Listen Up (10–15 minutes)

- Play each song for the class. (Note: The Bob Marley song mentions Jesus. If you use it, note for the students that people find inspiration from all religions to pursue fairness.) Ask: How do these songs relate to the actions of the heroes we've discussed?
- Ask: How can protest songs inspire us to make the world a fairer place? *(they can draw us in, help us feel what the musician is feeling, and motivate us to act)*

It's a Wrap! (5 minutes)

Ask: How can you follow the examples of the heroes we've discussed? Encourage students to think of personal situations that could be made fairer and how students might choose to act.

TAKING IT FURTHER

Memorial Design

Have students work in small groups to design memorials for Chaney, Goodman, and Schwerner. Students should think about what images or text the memorial should include, what it would be made of, and where it would be located. Encourage students to use their designs to inspire others to continue Chaney, Goodman, and Schwerner's work. Ask the groups to each make a rough sketch of their design to share with the class.

Lesson 3: How Can We Build Our Own Fairness Trait?

Learning Objectives: Students will:

- Explore how Jewish values can support acts of fairness in their daily lives.
- Explore ways that they can build their own fairness trait by practicing and supporting fairness.

LESSON ACTIVITIES

Getting Started: Facing (Un)Fairness (5–10 minutes)

Ask students to recall a time when they stepped in to do what they thought was fair, even though it was difficult. Ask: What were the challenges? How did you confront them? What were the results of your actions? If you had it to do over again, would you do anything differently? Be supportive of students who either have regrets or struggle to think of an example. Remind the class that facing unfairness isn't easy—otherwise, everyone would do it. Tell them they'll have a chance to brainstorm fairness strategies in this lesson.

Fairness in Action: Jacob Revels (5–10 minutes)

Ask: How is Jacob Revels making the world a fairer place? Have students work in pairs or small groups to find the answer in his profile on page 6 of the booklet. Ask the groups to discuss these questions and then share their ideas with the class:

- Jacob describes joining Or Tzedek as being a "first step" to making the world a better place. What other steps do you think he might take? *(he could volunteer, give money, or try to change laws to help solve the unfair problems he sees)* Which of these steps could you see yourself doing? How?
- Jacob chose an issue that he's passionate about—urban affairs in Chicago—and devoted himself to addressing it. Ask: What social issues are you passionate about? Remind students that everyone can make a difference, no matter how young.

Work Your Fairness Muscles (15–20 minutes)

- Divide students into small groups. Print and distribute information from fairness organizations, assigning one organization to each group. (Links can be found at www.behrmanhouse.com/hero.) Guide students to review the information and describe the organization's main goals in one or two sentences in their own words. Ask one volunteer per group to present these goals to the class.
- Allow students to vote, following the directions on page 6 of the booklet.
- Guide students to discuss their ideas of fairness within their groups. Encourage them to share personal experiences, if they're comfortable doing so. You may wish to provide an alternative activity, such as writing or drawing, to help students express their feelings about fairness more privately.

Superfair! (10–15 minutes)

- To introduce the activity on page 7 of the booklet, briefly discuss the history of Superman. Tell students that the character was created by two Jewish teenagers in the late 1930s. In early stories, he was particularly known for standing up for fairness and equality. (For more information about the Jewish origins of Superman, go to www.behrmanhouse.com/hero.)
- Have students work individually to design their superheroes and fairness equipment on page 7 of the booklet. Then have them go over the discussion questions in pairs or small groups.

Think About It (5 minutes)

Review the activity on page 8 of the booklet. Ask students to share their chosen words with their partner and the class, and list all the words on the board, a large sticky note, or other medium. Then review how these words apply to the actions of Ginsburg, Isaiah, other heroes, and the students themselves. *(respect; all of these heroes based their treatment of others on respect for them, and I try to do the same thing)*

Bringing Fairness Home (5–10 minutes)

- Review the activity on page 8 of the booklet. Ask students to interview a family member, a teacher, or another adult whom they trust. Encourage them to prepare what they've learned for the beginning of the next lesson.
- **Follow-Up:** Invite students to describe their interviews with the class. Ask: What did you learn that surprises you? If you were in the adult's shoes, would you have reacted the same way? Why or why not?

It's a Wrap! (5 minutes)

Ask: How does learning about *un*fairness strengthen your "fairness muscles"? Why is it so important to talk about injustice? Encourage students to reflect on the unfair situations they've discussed and the fairness heroes who addressed those situations.

TAKING IT FURTHER

Superhero Comics

Invite students to create comics using their fairness superheroes. Ask them to choose a scenario—from this booklet, Jewish history, or something they have seen or experienced—where something unfair happened or is happening. Then have them create a page or booklet of panels showing how their superhero's commitment to fairness could change the situation. Invite volunteers to present their comics to the class, and guide a discussion about the comics' real-world implications. Suggest that superheroes are not the only ones who can make the world fairer; these changes can happen if enough real people commit themselves to fairness.

Activities and Resources from the Museum

The Museum of the Jewish People at Beit Hatfutsot has a collection of exhibits and online resources with a wealth of information and stories about people—both famous and less well known—and communities from throughout the Jewish world. Here are some activity ideas and online resources from the museum to help learners further explore the heroes and themes developed in this book. More information about these resources can be found on page 42.

ACTIVITIES

Seder Table Hero

Ask students to browse the list of Jewish Nobel Prize winners on the Beit Hatfutsot website and come up with their own list of favorite Jewish heroes. Ask: If you could invite any of your heroes to your seder table, family dinner, or birthday party, who would you invite? Why? What questions would you ask them? Invite students to share their thoughts in small groups.

A Meeting of Heroes

Direct students to choose two or more heroes of different types from the Museum of the Jewish People app and imagine bringing them together for a meeting. What would they say to one another? What questions would they ask? What would they agree or disagree about? Students can then act out a skit, write a magazine article, or record an interview of this meeting.

Hero Elections

Have students choose one person from *all* the different heroes they learned about in this book and from their online research. Have students form small groups to debate their top choice of hero, and then have the class vote for the winner.

Heroes in My Life

Ask students: Who are your own personal heroes? Who do you know who embodies the traits we explored in this course: courage, kindness, creativity, curiosity, and fairness? Ask them to take a picture of the person and write a short description of why this person is a hero to them. If students want, they can upload their picture and description to the My Jewish Lens database on the Beit Hatfutsot website.

The Hero in Me

As a closing activity, ask students to browse the pictures and accompanying descriptions on the My Jewish Lens site, for a glimpse into the Jewish lives of people all over the world. Ask them to then take a photo of something they worked on during this course or of an object that represents their own character strengths or the hero they aspire to be. Have them write a short description and, if they choose, post it to the My Jewish Lens site.

RESOURCES FROM THE MUSEUM

Jewish Nobel Prize Winners

https://nobel.bh.org.il/en/

This online encyclopedia contains entries on all Jewish Nobel Prize winners throughout history. You can search the site by geographical location, year of award, or any search term. The winners of the Nobel Peace Prize are especially relevant for this course.

Museum of the Jewish People app

(search "BH Museum" in the app store)

This mobile app includes a visual guide and more information about the heroes featured in the "Trailblazers" gallery of the museum. Heroes are categorized by roles such as leaders, scientists, or revolutionaries.

My Jewish Lens

https://myjewishlens.bh.org.il/

My Jewish Lens is an international database of photos documenting the diversity of Jewish life, culture, and people around the world today. Anyone can submit a photograph with accompanying text and become a part of this living worldwide album.